MANIPULATION

How to Regain Control and Prevent Emotional Manipulation and Mind Control in Your Relationships

LEWIS FISCHER

Table of Contents

Introduction

The human mind is designed to be a part of a collective. As sophisticated as it is, it is designed to be malleable by its surroundings. That is a necessary condition for survival - malleability. A mind that is rigid will not be able to adapt to the changing environment. Imagine if a tree can only survive with sunshine the whole year. What happens in the winter – it dies. But what happens if that tree adapted to the climate - shed its leaves and 'hibernated' for the winter? It will survive and return in the spring. But the tree that didn't adapt to the change in season will wither and perish.

For the same reason, the mind has evolved to observe and adapt to its surroundings. It is able to detect the changes and the status of the world around it, and then to socialize, learn, experiment and mimic.

Mimicry and influence are two sides of the same coin. It is how we broadcast and receive intangible mindsets that determine everything from how we behave, how we think, what we chose, how we speak and so many more things that it is hard to believe that our so-called free will is not really free will.

When we adopt an idea or a method from someone else, we mimic them; when they follow us, we influence them. In some areas of life we influence, in many areas we mimic and that creates a class of influencers and a class of followers. This is normal – it is how a society forms, it is how our species and a number of other species behave. It is how we advance our primary purpose.

The human species is purposed to survive. The way it survives is to consume energy and nutrients, shelter itself from adverse elements – both physical and psychological, and create off spring so that it can extend from one generation to the next.

In short, to live and thrive along the unfolding of time, we have to roll with the punches and because our mind is the organ that determines that, our mind is naturally built to adapt. That adaptive quality has significant advantages – it allows societies to build in numbers and take on a character of its own. Have you ever been to a city and see the way the people are and go to a different city and find that the people there are totally different? The first time that became apparent to me was when I started travelling as a teenager, and I found that people were fundamentally different based on the country and city they lived in.

Even in the US you see that till today, New Yorkers behave differently from Californians, the North marches to a different beat than the South, and Middle America is different from Coastal America. The region, it turns out, molds us as much as we mold it.

Advantages aside, that malleability comes at a cost if we are not careful. In the world of psychographics, subliminal persuasion, and the influencer-follower relationship, the intent of the influencer takes deserves greater scrutiny because it is not always that the influencer is interested in the overall good, and sometimes is motivated by purse self-gain.

We will come back to this again later.

The other element of human character that is relevant to this topic is the fact that our fundamental nature of community is driven by equity. Equity is the fairness that determines the exchange of value. If a kid mows your lawn, you give him fifty bucks. When you work for your company, you are paid a just wage. You get the point

The principle of equity also covers the influencer-follower exchange. Look at it in modern terms. There are online influencers who are out there to evangelize the products they represent. In doing that, they highlight all the issues that are important to us about a product; and in return they are rewarded with a commission on sales or wages. The exchange is equitable.

Equity is the measure that is planted in the depths of our consciousness. We tend to understand what is fair and what is not. What is not within us is the empathy in sufficient quantities to project that balance of equity to our counterpart and see the equation from their perspective. In this scenario, it creates the possibility for us to push the boundaries and shortchange others.

Let me be clear, equity is not about equality. Equality is a different matter but not related to equity, especially in this context of value exchange. Equity is also something that is highly individual, and imposing our individual equity onto others is not wise. Think of it this way: A worker in China spends his day in a clothing factory earning $1 per day stitching hundreds of garments over the course of a month. We here in the US would not even consider that to be acceptable and may even view that as slave labor. But for the worker – he is more than happy to do it because it gives him a job to support himself and his family – no matter how humble the lifestyle. His alternative would be no job and life on the streets. Thus what we consider equitable is not equitable for them. That is a simple example to drive the point.

Or think about it this way. To be competitive, you lower your bid to beat out the higher-priced competitor. So you win the bid and now you have the job, but it is worth less - is that considered inequitable? No. So you see it's not the dollar-value that determines equity, it is the aggregate of the elements that make up your situation and that is a very personal and individual circumstance.

When someone robs another of that equity, there are two possible reasons. The first possibility is that the former's aggressive stance overpowers the latter's in the normal course of negotiation. The second is that the former intentionally brings external factors to bear in the execution of the negotiation.

Think of it this way. Two people negotiate the sale of land. The seller, armed with his own definition of equity wants a certain consideration; the buyer armed with his definition of equity wants something different. The two negotiate and go back and forth and eventually the balance is struck. However, if the buyer kidnaps the seller's child, and demands a more advantageous price as consideration – he has brought in an external factor and tilted the scales of equity. He has used a powerful element of fear to sway the normal course of equitable negotiation. Aside from being distasteful, it is of course illegal – but it is just used here are an example to drive the point.

This external element to tilt the scales of equity is typically related to one of the motivating factors of the human species - primarily fear. We will look at fear in a little more detail as the book stretches its legs. But for now you must understand that fear is a key motivator in a lot of the things that we do. Whether that fear is warranted or it is a misfire in our synapses, the result is the same. We move fervently to correct the situation that triggers that fear, and if that is not possible, we cut off the feeling or the sense that is responsible for triggering that fear. It's like being in a plane and an alarm or warning triggers – if you can't fix it, at least disengage the alarm so that it stops distracting you. The same thing happens here.

We have looked at three elements thus far: influence, equity, and fear. We can see why all are necessary for the proper functioning of this species and the functioning of our individual self. So how does emotional manipulation fit in with all this?

The three elements we briefly touched on and introduced are natural parts of your psyche and our physiology. Emotional manipulation occurs when the influencer applies undue methods, like fear, to get the victim to commit an act that is not equitable, in part or completely. That's the simple definition, but it carries a lot of baggage that deserves to be expanded on and explained.

That is, in part, what we shall do over the course of this book.

Chapter 1: Introduction to Emotional Manipulation

Emotional Manipulation is the use of emotion (particularly fear) to do something against your will but you are stuck in this untenable position and you know that you will feel horrible for doing something that is in your best interest if it goes against their wishes.

Just as you can be subject to emotional manipulation, it is also possible that you unknowingly and unwittingly subject your loved ones, or someone close to you, or even a stranger if your gravity is strong enough, to emotional manipulation. This book is going to look at the subject from both ends of the spectrum – from the person who manipulates knowingly for his own ends, to the person who manipulates without realizing it and not for his own benefit.

The Manipulation Framework

The manipulation framework is a theoretical profile that can be used to get a better grasp of the subject matter. It gives the reader a three dimensional perspective of three key elements in emotional manipulation and on the severity of the situation and the distinction between an equitable situation and an accidental one.

Intent

Imagine that to be the first axis and it is laid out horizontally. It makes up the first dimension of manipulation and it has to do with the intent and knowledge of the manipulator. Intent of the aggressor is a key factor in this and the intention is not to explicitly premeditate the manipulation of the victim, but rather the intent defines the willingness to take advantage of the person without regard to the person's eventual state.

I believe we should always leave a person with the same equity we find them in, or better. Most times, if done right, relationships yield synergies that result in both parties better off than they would have been if they never partook in the relationship. But this is ideal and in many scenarios, one party is always left holding the chaff and the other party walks away with the wheat.

Coming back to the role of intent on manipulation.

Whether someone intends to manipulate you or otherwise is immaterial. You have to look at it and ask yourself if you are manipulating someone or you are being manipulated by someone. In this scenario, identifying the manipulation gets harder and determining the intent behind it gets more obscure.

Relationship

Now imagine the second axis that measures the relationship between the parties – think of it as the vertical axis and one end measures the closeness of the manipulator and the victim. One end of the spectrum is that the two are strangers (like two people who just met), and the other end where they have known each other for ages, are likely married or living together, might even be related – as in filial manipulation. There is evidence that mothers tend to be emotionally manipulative over one or more of their daughters in different ways.

Gravity

The third axis that rounds out the matrix gives real insight and puts us on the path to a solution to the whole thing is the gravity to the manipulation. Gravity is not about the strength of the manipulation, it is about the initiating source. It is often taken for granted that the manipulator is the initiator of the problem and the victim is the helpless target. That is not always the case. There are cases where the same person is manipulated wherever he or she goes and is the victim of various manipulators. In cases like this you should start to questions the victim, and when you do you start to identify the traits that go into the profile of a victim. You will see that sometimes victims have so much gravity that they seek out and attract manipulators or they make a person manipulate them. So when you look at a situation where one is manipulating the other you cannot just jump to the conclusion that the victim has nothing to do with it.

Some victims find their strength in being a victim. It is their own psychology and in some cases it may be an unhealthy relationship, and in other cases both parties get what they want. One gets to be in control and extract benefit, and the other gets to be the martyr.

Having said that, I must address the issue that some people might think that I am about to place blame of the emotional manipulation on the victim and reduce the burden of responsibility of the belligerent.

That is not the case at all. What it is done for is to highlight the realities that a prospective victim might exhibit or the ways an unwitting manipulator might take on. After all, human beings, sociopathic or empathetic, are driven by the balance of interaction and selfish purpose of self-betterment. It is a natural tendency that goes overboard and becomes unhealthy. In the case of an overbearing manipulator, this selfish desire has taken an unhealthy turn; and in the case of the un-realizing victim, they have the mistaken notion that they have nothing else to offer in turn for what they want – be it misguided expression of care, or the misguided definition of love.

Intervention

The three axes we listed form the framework of the emotionally manipulative relationship. Those who see it in the aggressor, would intervene and highlight it to them lest they are not aware; and those who see it in the victim, certainly should bring it up because they are definitely unaware of their behavior and their options.

Getting out of this dynamic starts with the recognition of the matter, then followed by a self-reflective analysis of the factors at play and ends with the courage to make the necessary decisions.

If the person doing the analysis is the person in the relationship, it is best to start with yourself than with the shortcomings of the counterpart. If you are an outsider looking in, then you should look carefully at the dynamic at play before you offer any advice. External advice beyond telling the aggressor or the victim that there is emotional manipulation at play should not be taken lightly and then once the decision is made to voice it, it should be strictly limited to making it known. How to go about it and what to do should be avoided.

The unintended consequence of stressing the matter too much can be disastrous. So tread carefully. Remember constantly that the road to hell is paved with good intentions. Your good intention may make things worse than it already is.

Advancing the Manipulation Framework

With that said, it is time to dive into the three axes of emotional manipulation and find where any instance of manipulation sits within that framework. The reason we want to use this framework will become clear as we proceed. But for those of you who already get an idea you will see that the more close the relationship, the higher the intersection of the three factors shift towards; and the more gravity that is displayed the more forward it moves. And the more right it moves in terms of intent where the aggressor is impressing more intention to extract benefit from the victim, the more to the right the intersection moves. This quadrant is the most obvious and those in this quadrant will most likely already know it in their hearts that manipulation is afoot, or has a high probability of settling into the relationship.

Why do we want to understand it in these terms? Because manipulation is complex and you need to start with a framework that is not biased, and one that gets you started on the right road. If you just happen to fall into it or you are just finding out because your instincts are telling you so or a friend has alerted you to the matter, then you need a good framework to wrap your head around this issue.

So with that let us start with the first axis of intent.

The two extremes of this axis as you can imagine are that of total ignorance of the fact or total premeditation of it. It is completely possible that a person is ignorant of the fact that they are being manipulated and it is also totally possible that a person does it without realizing it.

Manipulation is the extension of getting what you want from a person when you believe that they are not going to easily give it up. Who among us has not been guilty of getting what you want by doing or saying anything to get someone to do something. My sister-in-law married a guy who told her that he was a millionaire. He wasn't. She married him under those conditions and later lived a regular life. She swears constantly in jest that she was manipulated into marriage. That's not really something we would consider manipulation. My wife and I placed broccoli and carrots in front of our kids – that convinced them to do something that most kids don't do. Is that manipulation? My best friend's wife bakes him his favorite apple pie and gets him his favorite tobacco pipe when she wants to go shopping? Is that manipulation? They all fit the definition, but they are not manipulation, are they?

There is something missing in the classical definition of getting what you want out of a person, and it is not just intent, it goes beyond intent and when you visualize this axis, you should include this in factoring the depth of intention. It has to be a brand of malicious intent that is persistent to the point that the other person is not going to put up a defense because there is no overt sign of force or definable characteristic of their actions that suggests manipulation.

The reason this happens is because the human mind is very good at identifying individual features but when you put them all together, it is almost unrecognizable. You get hints and notions of something stirring, but it is hard to determine and for those who do not have the confidence to rely on their inclinations, the whole picture remains a blur and unrecognizable. That does not mean that humans are stupid and it certainly does not mean that victims of manipulation are daft. It's just that we do not know what to look for and so it is unrecognizable to us. We have to be shown a pattern or at least taught how to find the sting in our hearts, and when we tug on that string, our own subconscious will eventually allow the real picture to come into focus. And that will confirm for us that we are being manipulated.

We tend to think of manipulation as something that is obvious, deliberate and menacing. It can be, it doesn't have to be and it rarely has all three of those in its execution. If it did, those would be easily recognizable and you could put a stop to it instantly. But what we are talking about here is the kind that is subtle, possibly inadvertent, and almost always never menacing. But the effects can be disastrous nonetheless.

Psychological Effects of Manipulation

What are the effects of manipulation? Well primarily, the effect is one that alters your way of doing something and then changing your frame of reference to fit the change. That has psychological consequences. Manipulation is about getting you to do something that you don't already want to do or would not have considered and puts you at a disadvantage. If you don't know how you got there, the psychological consequence of being duped can be extensive especially if it is one that lasts over a long period of time. Ironically, the longer you face it and the longer you are subjected to it then it gets to a point that you confidence level erodes and the ability to stand up to something gets worse. Eventually it molds you into subservience and the inability to function normally. This is just one strand of the complicate web of manipulation effects.

Chapter 2:
Who Has the Influence

The human mind is so malleable that it can be made to do anything, even things that are against one's own self-interest. This design allows us to do a number of things and have a number of things done to us. If you want to understand how the basic mind works, all you need to do is observe a child. Children are easily influenced because their minds are altered in respect to the thing that they are being influenced about.

I will give you a simple example. My wife and I conducted an innocuous experiment with our kids when they were young. When our first arrived, and was still on milk, he would sit at the table with us during meals and there would always be a dish of broccoli and carrots at the table and we made it a point to relish it while we ate, and always finished it. No matter what was on the table besides that, meat, potatoes, beans, whatever – there would always be broccoli and carrots. We never tried to feed it to him, we never forced him, and never introduced it to him, but we scarfed it down at every meal – it was always the first thing we reached for.

When he turned 5 months old, we noticed that he would intently watch us as we sat down for the meal and he would mimic the chewing. We never forced him to switch to solid food. He was always breast fed and we let him make his choice. We figured he would tell us when he was ready for solids.

His first signal was that he would mimic chewing after watching us at every meal. As a starter we introduced him to mashed potatoes and he would flap his gums just as he had mimicked us in the past – he did really love it and was really excited. But something else happened. He started to reach for the broccoli and carrots. I have never known any kid who ate their broccoli after being hounded by concerned parents, much less voluntarily. Fast forward 18 years and he still loves his broccoli and insists on having it whenever he comes home from college.

We thought maybe that was one off, so we tried it again with our second, and our third. All three of them eat their broccoli, carrots and along the way we added a few other vegetables to the list.

That as an important parenting guide for us. We never strike our kids, or raise our voice at them. We have conversations and so it's not always easy to converse a kid into doing something. So what we decided to do was teach by example. In doing so two things happen – we thought them what to do by using the internal desire to mimic and we learnt as parents there are a scary number of things out there that could influence our kid.

Let me explain.

The idea of doing this with the broccoli and carrots came about when we were talking about TV programs and kids in general. We were talking about how these kids mimicked what they saw on TV and how crazy it was to let that garbage enter a vulnerable kid's mind. It slowly dawned on us that the absorption of an act or behavior was not limited to bad acts or bad habits, they were for all things. So we just decided to change the paradigm and cut out the poor examples and enrich them with the good examples.

The results worked out I am happy to say.

The point is that you can influence a kid to do anything. You don't need to scream at them (in fact screaming at them and forcing them to do things actually doesn't work as well as you would imagine).

Instead you can get them to do things that they may not know to do or may otherwise not want to do. When it comes to your kids, as long as it is in their best interest, you can't call that manipulation. But it is exactly that when the person you are doing it to is an adult – your contemporary, your colleague, your significant other or whatever the relationship – even if they are strangers. When you intentionally do something to make someone do something that benefits you (materially or psychologically) and that is not directly known to the person whereby he or she can chose to accept the direction or deny.

The point of this book is to look at manipulation and guide the conversation around the elements of psychological manipulation and emotional manipulation. To be clear, we are not talking so much about a stated threat that leads someone to do something. That is a form of manipulation, but, more appropriately, that is an explicit threat. It is more appropriate to call that duress. Emotional manipulation and psychological manipulation are different for this and cause you to do the thing that you ordinarily would not do because you have a fear of the repercussion by the aggressor.

Manipulation is more insidious because it uses your evolved faculties of imagination and fear. It is dangerous, more than any other form of control, because the victim either can't tell they are being manipulated, or know it and can't extricate themselves from it.

Intangible manipulation has two veins. The first is psychological, the other is emotional. The psychological manipulation is the one that they don't know they are being manipulated and the emotional manipulation is the one where they may not know it, but even after they do, they can't get out. We will start with psychological manipulation and then move on to emotional manipulation because they both have common roots and similar effects but have distinct differences when it comes to recognizing, preventing, and neutralizing it.

Psychological manipulation is what you see in advertisements that make you do things that you don't already want to do especially when it is against your best interest. You do the bidding and then you have no remorse over it as you are totally on board.

The main target – the jugular of the matter, is the person's fear. A good example of psychological manipulation is the recent Brexit vote in the United Kingdom – the vote to leave the European Union. The run-up to the referendum was an amazing study in psychographics and psychological manipulation.

Remember that we said earlier that influence is the relationship between the influencer and the follower. We automatically give credibility to those who have authority. Technological products – like search engines, and social networks try to assign authority to individuals based on popularity. And that is a good place to start when it comes to interpersonal relationship over electronic networks.

Determining which has the influence will give you a good picture of the potential of the manipulation. The person without the influence is not able, by definition to be able to manipulate the other. So instead of recognizing manipulation, start with trying to recognize the person with the greater power to influence in the relationship.

Power

In interpersonal relationships, power is the term that is assigned to the person who has the ability to make the other person do what the first person wants even if and when he doesn't want to. The more the relative dislike the more the power. Think about that this way, as an illustration.

If one kid tells the other kid to do his homework (something that is really unpleasant and complicated) the kid is not going to do it because he really doesn't want to. In this case the first kid has no power over the other kid.

Taking that same dynamic, but if you make it a scenario between a kid and his parent, then when the parent tells the kid to do his homework, the kid does it. That describes the power the parent has over the kid. But this is a very innocent and mutually beneficial power. But this is not manipulation because it does not leave the child in a worse of position after the deed is done.

Now look at a third relationship. You just meet a stranger and they make you do something that you don't want to do, and once the deed is done it leaves you in a worse state than before you met, and you received nothing in return. Don't confuse this for emotional manipulation just yet. I am merely trying to exhibit the various shades of power. In this scenario, the person has a power over you.

Power is a funny thing. It is not absolute. Just because you have power doesn't mean you can wield it onto anyone. Power is only exercisable in comparison. That means one must have greater power over the other before it can be used. Remember power is described or defined as the ability to make someone do something that they ordinarily wouldn't do. We are not quite ready to match this to emotional manipulation, because those with power could emotionally manipulate someone, but those who emotionally manipulate someone are not always powerful.

An example of that would be if the victim was empathic. AN empath is someone who absorbs more emotion that a typical person. If they can sense tremendously more than anyone else then the slighted detection that the other person would like you to do something for them will be magnified and they would go about doing it just so as to not feel bad about it. This does not mean the other person has the power over the empath.

This relates back to the issue of gravity in the manipulation axis. If you recall, gravity describes the person who has the ability to attract manipulators or the manipulator who has the ability to attract victims – in essence, it is the dynamic between a person who is naturally a victim, a person who is naturally a manipulator and the combination of two people who, without the presence of each other, would not be victim or manipulator, but when they meet naturally fall into that kind of a relationship.

It is important to know which way the gravity moves things. If you can't see the gravitational forces, then you will not be able to recognize your own state in the dynamic. This brings us back to the power.

When two natural manipulators come together, there is a clash. When two natural victims come together there is no pain, but it is still unhealthy.

Power is a component of manipulation, but not the only component. Intelligent and sensitive people have power but they do not use it to manipulate others. The person who does the manipulation is the one that has greater comparative power and is unable to get what he wants in mutual agreement or thought other means and rests to underhanded tactic which usually results in manipulation.

To neutralize the emotional manipulation, you have to stop caring what the other person says or feels. This balances the power they have over you. Power to compel action using external force is not emotional manipulation – and if you believe that physical harm may result from denial of request by the aggressor then you have a problem greater than emotional manipulation and beyond the scope of this book. But the power to compel you from within you is emotional manipulation. That gives you two alternatives. The first it can either weaken you out, or it can make you realize that you have the ultimate power over what goes on inside. Don't let anyone on the outside to dictate what goes on inside.

Ultimately only you have the power of your own destiny and you need to make it a habit to remember that.

Frame of Mind

Not to sound sexist, but women are usually on the receiving end of manipulation. That can be stopped if you decide to. But to do that you have to alter the strength of your mind and do it in a way that is more aggressive than it is defensive.

Recently a group of researchers conducted two tests to illustrate how powerful seemingly innocuous events can shape our mind. They went to Harvard University and chose two hundred undergraduates and administered a math test. They broke the group up randomly in to two groups consisting of male and female students. They administered the same test except they changed the first question for the two groups.

For the first group, the first question asked them about their gender followed by regular math questions. To the second group the questions were a set of regular math problems. When they scored the exam, the women in the first group (the group that had answered the question about their gender), scored an average of ten points lower than the guys in that first group while the women in the second group (who were not asked about their gender) scored the same as the men in the second group. Put a pin in that for a minute. I will come back to that shortly.

In another experiment researchers went out randomly into the crowd at a mall, and walked up to them and asked them for a favor. The pretense was that they needed help with their cup of coffee while they took out their keys from their pocket. Most strangers obliged. And that was the end of it. They sampled about 200 people, making sure that these people held a cup of coffee (either hot or cold) for at least 20 seconds.

Those people were tracked and a little while later another person would approach them and would request these people to take a random survey in exchange for $20. Most people obliged as it was a fairly short survey.

What they found is relevant to our book here. Those people that were given coffee to hold, were separated into two groups. The first group, was given a cold cup, while the second was given a warm cup.

Those same people when surveyed were asked to describe a celebrity that everyone would know. The answers they gave were categorized and fell almost exactly along the lines of the coffee cup's temperature. That is to say, those who held a warm cup of coffee for 20 seconds wrote warmly about the subject, those who helped an ice-cold cup wrote a rather cold review instead.

There are numerous other tests that prove the thesis that our minds are more malleable than we realize and that results in the way our minds create our personalities. In the first test all those who answered the gender question were reminded of their stereotypes and instantly that altered their ability. That test does not propose that women are less capable then men, it proves that the stereotype we have of the gender differences causes us to behave differently at a subconscious level that can even turn our intellect on and off. It is the same when it comes to being manipulated. It is more prevalent that women are more empathic and the softer side of the equation. Nothing wrong with that, but when you remind someone that that is who they are, they take on the stereotypes and then they become easier to manipulate.

Being told that you are beautiful, sexy, gorgeous are all ways that lead to a certain form of weakening of your intellect and those results in the path to manipulation. Well, not all times but it can be. Men tend to pay obsequious complements to women so that they can take advantage of the situation. It is not the complement that breaks them, but the reminder that they are women in conjunction with the complement.

Just like the experiment with the hot cup of coffee and the warm reviews, the human mind that is ignorant of its own weakness can be manipulated without hope of putting up a defense. The very first step in the manipulation process starts with the words a person speaks. You need to be able to recognize it and return the gesture or put a stop to it.

Your frame of mind needs to be strengthened before the event. It's like building the walls to a medieval city. You don't erect the walls just when the marauding armies arrive you build them ahead of time.

The other thing that you have to do is alter the stereotype that you have of your gender and yourself. Once you neutralize that, it's harder for anyone to use that to get you to submit. If you look at the art of enslaving people, even till today, a few slave owners can control hundreds of slaves. Why? Can't the slaves overpower them with numbers? No, because their frame of mind has been manipulated and their mind has submitted,

Protect your mind and your thoughts and you will be able to fend off a large part of the manipulating aggressor.

Keeping the Fantasy Alive

Most manipulative situations are never real. I am not saying that the manipulation is not real – it is very real indeed. I am saying that the illusion that the manipulator creates so that the victim will fall in line is based on things that are not real.

Manipulators are structurally weak but have the power on the outside to dictate the terms of the engagement. Think about that for a minute. A person who is not strong would need to resort to manipulative means to make up for what they think they are missing.

Why do people cheat in business and politics? Because they don't have the game at the level they need to be to beat the opponent or the competitor. Why do students cheat on exams? Because they are not up to the mark when it comes to having the level of knowledge they need to make the grade. People do underhanded things when they believe they do not have what it takes to get what they want. Manipulation is the same. Psychographic manipulation is the same when it comes to advertising. Inferior products advertise in unscrupulous ways to be able to convince their audience that their product is better when it really is not. Or even when their product is good but they are fighting against another product that is equally good, manipulative advertising is used to rob us of the choices we would have made by messing with our heads.

If you can realize for a second that the power of the manipulation doesn't lie within the aggressor but within you, you may feel like you are to blame for it, but it is not about blame. It is about power. If you take control of the manipulative process and disallow the external hand to come in and move your pieces around, then you will be all the better for it.

Power through Apparent Weakness

In the last section we looked at the victims of manipulation in terms of gender and why the potential for manipulation exists to a greater degree. But that does not mean in any way that emotional manipulation does not happen in the state of weakness. That is why we specifically looked at the potential gravity a person has when we looked at the manipulation framework. A weaker person can be manipulated to do things they won't do because of the other person's ability to manipulate but sometimes the reverse is true when the person uses their weakness as the tool to manipulate.

Because we have a sense of decency and kindness we would not choose to deny the request of someone who is in apparent difficulty. I travelled to a third world country some time ago and spent some time in one of its bustling cities that had droves of homeless people and a very high poverty rate. There were panhandlers everywhere and because the competition among pan handlers were so high that they resorted to emotional manipulation.

There were many strategies but the most common was to use cripple children by their side and panhandle for money. The cripple children were almost never their children. They just used them and hardly paid them for it. The visual of seeing an adult carrying a cripple child asking for money is gut wrenching to those who are not used to such visuals. That is being emotionally manipulative from a point of weakness. They prey on your kindness and common human decency.

It is so apparent that even when you get to the point that you know that you are being taken advantage of, you still give in. That is the ultimate in emotional manipulation.

But there are also other forms of manipulation though weakness and it can span short games or long games (you will see what this means in Chapter 3). The only way to get through this kind of manipulation is to understand your own perceptions and your own view on things that make you uncomfortable. That means, you have to put a full stop at being controlled into helping someone. You should instead make it a habit to help a person on your own time in your own way.

Let me give you an example. When I was approached the first time in this town, I took everything I had in my pocket that was denominated in the local currency and gave it to the person who was holding this crippled child. But then a friend of mine who was familiar with the neighborhood told me what was really going on and so I learned and decided to not put up to being manipulated.

The next time it happened to me, I was approached by a man who had a little blind girl in tow and he was dragging her along. The difference is that I smelled a strong whiff of alcohol. And he came over and asked for money and said that it was to feed his daughter. If it was indeed his daughter, she indeed looked to be undernourished. Instead of giving him cash, I walked into a convenience store right behind us and came out with a bag of food and gave it to him.

He tried telling me that he didn't want that and only wanted cash, which my companion translated for me. I pretended not to understand and gave him the bag of food anyway. I thought I got around it. But as soon as I walked away, he went straight into the convenience store and traded the food (I left the receipt in the bag) for liquor. I should have known better but my mind was still clouded by the emotional manipulation that I was being subjected to by the visual of this little girl.

So I went back to the convenience store bought some food – enough for just the little girl who was sitting by his side, and gave it to her. And told her to eat it while I stood there watching. The moment she had taken a few bites, I left – I don't think the guy could use half eaten food.

The point that I am laboring to make is that emotional manipulation can come in many forms, weakness is one. It can really pull on your heart stings but you have to look at what is real and not give in to the apparent emotional effect that the displayed weakness is supposed to illicit.

One way to prevent emotional manipulation is to do things in your own way in your own time and not in response to what others try to profit from you.

Another element that you would want to keep not of is the gravity field between you and any one person that comes across. Manipulation, in any form, is a function of relative strength. It is like the power voltage in a circuit where current flows from a greater power to a lesser one. The difference is called a power potential.

Power Potential

The power potential is akin to a water fall. Water will fall from a higher ground to the lower ground naturally. There are two ways the force of that water can be increased or decreased. The first is if you were to increase the height of the fall, then the water will fall with more force. You can think of this part of the analogy as the difference between powers. The second way to increase the power potential is to increase the gravity. If the gravity is significantly higher than even a short difference in height between the higher ground and the lower ground would yield a powerful difference.

The power potential between two people is almost the same way. For the manipulator to emotionally manipulate the victim there must be a huge power potential. Either the person is significantly more powerful or the victim as a much higher gravity.

The person with the greater power potential has the greater influence over the person with the lesser.

The best way to detect if manipulation could be an issue is to look at this power potential. You will see this across a large variety of relationships. You see this in cases where people of power have uncommon power over people who work for them. Their emotional manipulation is not just a function of the powerful influencer taking the power, it is also a function of the weaker giving the stronger the power to manipulate – it is the homage of acquiescence.

To be able to stave off emotional manipulation requires that you change this power potential. You can do one or both of the things that you see contribute to the differential. The way to do this is to strengthen your mind and to avoid falling prey to the stereotype of your situation. If you are less wealthy than another person, remove wealth from the equation. Do not see yourself in terms of wealth. If you see the other person to be more charming, then either you advance your charm, or you extricate charm from the equation. If you are dominated by wit, then turn silent. No level of wit in the world can penetrate the shield of silence. If all else fails, walk away.

The power potential is at play in all relationships. From father and son, to husband and wife, best friends, between lovers, and among strangers in a bar. You just have to figure out which arena it is in with a particular person and then apply the appropriate antidote.

Once you can recognize the power potential and apply the antidote, you are half way out of manipulation's grip.

Chapter 3:
How to Tell if You're Being Manipulated

Manipulation is about survival. The one who is manipulated fears something in the situation that is a threat to his or her survival and the person who is doing the manipulation is doing so because he or she thinks that it is advancing their survival. It really boils down to that.

Think long and hard about it and you will find that it indeed does all comes down to survival. Animals fight for territory because of survival. Humans fight for politics because of survival. But that perspective of survival is not always true because what they perceive and what really is, is never the same.

Your interest is in survival but being the subject of manipulation is not going to advance the elements of survival – it will eventually diminish it in the long term. Let's look at a hypothetical scenario, just to drive the point. If you know the relationship is manipulative, then you should also know that the person has all the power. But you're ok with that because you have something in return – the suppression of your greater fears – perhaps the fear of being alone, or the fear of confrontation or something more. You make the conscious decision that the manipulation is acceptable because the consideration you receive foe that manipulation is acceptable – or at least you grow into that. But what happens if one day that person does the exact thing that you are afraid – and let's say, leaves you. Now what has happened is that you are crushed, robbed, of your strength and alone.

Nothing is worth being manipulated over. But you can't fight that person who is manipulating you. You have only two ways to handle this. You either let the person know that you are feeling manipulated or you get yourself out from under.

Easier said than done. I know,

The thing that you need to learn, above all else is the art of knowing when you are being manipulated. With respect to time, there are two kinds of manipulation strategies that you need to be aware of. There is the one-off manipulation that someone does to make sure they get something they ant. The second one is the long horizon perpetual manipulation where you slowly but surely capitulate in many different areas.

We will look at both in turn and show you how to recognize the patterns to understand if you are being manipulated.

Short Game

The short game refers to the one-off manipulation strategies and it is basically somebody wanting something that you otherwise would not give. There is a lot of this going on and you could look at this from the perspective of the aggressor or the perspective of the victim. I am going to look exclusively at the perspective of the victim and especially the kind of victim that keeps getting manipulated by more than one person and many times in their life.

You can think of the person as a push over, or a person who is just a glutton for punishment. I am not talking about people who lose their money to scammers or people who get cheated by travelling salesmen. I am talking about the kind of person that is so easy to manipulate because they just want to be accepted or they just want to be liked.

The first thing that you have to recognize in the art of manipulation is not to look at the guy a mile away, but to look at yourself in the mirror. There are people who are going to immediately jump and say that it is in bad taste to point the finger at the victim. But we are not here to point the finger at the victim, we are here to protect the victim. You need to stop yourself from playing the victim and start learning how to stand up for yourself.

Manipulators are everywhere. You can't change all of them or punish all of them, you can only protect yourself. Look at it this way. Imagine if you were the King of a country and there are twenty other countries around you and all of them have nuclear weapons. Which is easier? Are you convincing them to dismantle their missiles? Or, are you getting your own missiles? Nuclear proliferation issues aside, you get the point?

Ten Steps to Survive the Short Game

The only true way to survive in this world and to thrive in it is to bolster yourself and to keep yourself on the cutting edge of self-improvement.

As such we now come to the first thing that you have to do to get yourself fortified so that others don't mark you as a target and you don't succumb to their methods. Your disposition should be that you are affable to everyone but you are no one's fool and as such you always look at the possibility that any request out of the ordinary, and act out of the norm, or any gesture beyond boundaries is a warning sign that you should just rebuff any contact.

That's your first act.

Your second act is to never concede defeat. A person who misses a step and then festers over it is a person who is a target for future episode. Here is an example. Let's say someone manipulates you into lending them money. They use all kinds of emotional tactics and you give in. Sometime later this person and your money, vanish. The thing you shouldn't do is go on about how you got duped. You should turn it around and stand up and say you did it knowing that the person was going to do this and that the money was not a big deal. But internally, you should learn how you fell for the emotional manipulation and not let that happen again.

There are two reasons for this, the more you beat yourself up externally, the more you set yourself up to be a target, and the more you damage yourself psychologically. You have to turn each assault into your advantage, and learning is the best advantage.

Never advertise that you have been victimized.

The third is that you can learn from mistakes before it becomes a pattern. You can see people a mile away that are going to take advantage of your state. Have you ever heard the thing about how guys look for one night stands with girls who are vulnerable because they just broke up – that's emotionally manipulative. Have you ever seen women who manipulate men into dong what they don't want to do by suggesting suicide – that's manipulative. These may not be anything that you are faced with, or things that you do – and that's not the point. But you see the use of heart strings in making someone else do something that they don't want to do – before the event and during the event. Psychological manipulation is a little different – that's when you alter their way of thinking into doing something and even if they didn't want to do it before they heard the pitch, they were more than willing to do it after and didn't feel like they were forced to do it.

Look at the difference – it is subtle and it is almost imperceptible. It is one that you can't really define but you know it's there. That's why emotional manipulation is so egregious – because it is so insidious.

The next thing, that you need to do to detect if there is emotional manipulation, is to trust your instincts. It is safe to say that you should never allow anyone into your emotional side until you find that they have passed all the criteria that you have put in place. It's like letting someone into your home. If you let someone in and they take your stuff, you have no on to blame but yourself. At least that is a good way to look at it. Of course there are those who would say that most people don't do that and you should not keep yourself castled within your own heart. But that is not the case. That only holds for the person who is not the kind that others see as someone that could be manipulated. If you find that more than one person comes along and manipulates you for one thing or another, then you need pull up the drawbridge, drop the gates and lock up the castle. Unless that person has the secret handshake and password, they don't get to pass.

The fourth thing is that you should always fend for yourself and never allow someone to get away with something because you need the friendship, or you need someone to like you. You do not need anyone to like you and you certainly do not need to purchase that affection.

Your fifth step is to listen and remember. Most manipulators can be found out very easily if you take the effort to listen to everything they have to say and remember it because in time, it won't make sense. Manipulation is not righteous and thus the facts will never hold up in daylight. A person who is constantly lying or lying in key areas – especially if their lies are close to the truth, then you need to be very careful – but that is also most prominent with the long game players which we will look at in the next section. But for the short game, manipulators lie close to the truth and are never sincere. If you take the effort to listen and remember, you will be able to detect their kind.

You don't have to call them out on their lies or deceit – but you just need to move away as quickly as you can. This is so you do not get into an untenable situation or a trap.

The sixth thing you got to watch out for is the trap. Emotional manipulators are looking for the opportunity to spring a trap on you and it is an emotional trap. They want to get you emotionally indebted to them or they want you to owe them, so they may go out of the way to offer you a favor and then manipulate your sense of gratitude in order to extract what they want. To be clear, in life, there are lots of quid pro quo situations, but emotional manipulation is not that. It is about trapping you then extracting what they want by reminding you that you owe them or triggering your sense of decency or guilt.

The seventh thing to watch for and overcome is the pity-manipulator. They are looking to lean on your sense of empathy. You will notice that most people who are manipulated – like the ones in chapter one where we talked about gravity – those who are empathic or have sensitive constitutions are easily manipulated because they thrive on your pity and they can extract whatever they want because they can spark the sense of pity in you and you will do what they want even though you don't want to because the pain of not complying is too much. This is why you have to block any outward emotion of what affects you and what pulls you down.

The eighth step to survive is recognizing the pattern of manipulators. They always want something for nothing, or they want something that is inequitable – meaning that you give up significantly more than they do, emotionally. If the relationship is new and they want a huge favor and they use guilt, pity, or gratitude to extract it from you then, on principle you should decline. Better to feel guilty in the short run than to be emotionally manipulated.

The ninth one is the manipulation by a friend who you've known for some time. Familiarity sometimes does breed contempt and sometimes when they want something they forget the bedrock friendship and they manipulate you based on the loss of friendship if you don't come through for them. This is in all of our DNAs. Kids do that to other kids. Since young they grow up using their friendship as a threat and saying they won't be your friend if you don't do something for them. Even if you were the kind to capitulate back then, don't do it now. Even if you understand their position, never capitulate.

Finally, you can identify the short game manipulator by the shift in the nature of his approach. An emotionally manipulative gesture starts with a break in routine behavior − if this person is known to you. You will also have noticed that they have manipulated others in front of you and they do it without realizing that they are manipulating. Most manipulators are not conscious of their own actions, they just want something for nothing and are sociopathic in the way they go about. If you see someone manipulate others watch them carefully and keep your drawbridge up when they are around.

Many of the short game strategies can happen in the long game as well as we will soon see.

Long Game

Although we refer to this as the long game, I assure you there is nothing fun about this. The long game is about the manipulation that happens over years and it is one that is as corrosive as it is insidious. When the game is said and done the victim is left sapped of their confidence and their state of mind. Much of the rest of the book is dedicated to the skills and strategies to look within yourself to overcome the power of the long game and the typical manipulator.

The long game occurs over years and could be one that happens in a marriage, in a long term relationship, between parents and children, between siblings, or even between classmates. It is dangerous because the victim is more emotionally vested that in the short game. It is also worst that the short game because it could either mean that the victim is stuck and in fear or it could mean that the manipulation will end in a very bad state.

In the first scenario, the victim could be manipulated and know it but the level of fear is significant that he or she cannot extricate themselves from it. The second one is that the victim has become so dependent on the manipulator that it is easier to be manipulated than it is to leave. What's worse is a variation of this scenario, where the relationship has become co-dependent and the manipulator still wields power over the victim. In this case the stress can increase because the manipulator needs to extract more in return for less.

Ten Ways to Overcome the Long Game

The first lesson of avoiding the long game is to not let the short game evolve into a long one. Make sure you do not entertain any hesitancy in walking away from a short game and make sure that it doesn't evolve into a long one. Sometimes if manipulators find that they can get more out of an easy prey so they extend their horizon.

The second lesson is to make sure you have set your own rules. You need to keep your boundaries and respect other's boundaries as well. If you are in a situation where boundaries are being violated you need to make it clear. Sometimes boundaries are breached unintentionally and this can then become a habit and then what happens is that the victim becomes an accidental victim and the manipulator becomes an accidental manipulator. The best thing to do is to air it out as soon as you feel something is not to your comfort.

The third lesson is to never allow penetration of those boundaries until you are good and ready. Breaching boundaries is a major issue in long term relationships. If you are in a relationship where there are no boundaries then you need to create some where it matters most.

The fourth is the moving of these boundaries. Do not compromise your boundaries in a way that you move them just because they were breached. You have to hold on to these boundaries no matter how close you are to this person. It is almost a pipe dream to think that a person should just meld their minds into yours and the two become one. That does not happen all the time and that does not happen when one party is weaker than the other. Look at it this way, would you want to meld your mind to someone weaker than you, and manipulators always see their victims as weak. They have no intention of becoming one with you; their only intention is to make use of you to the furthest extent that you allow them to. A real romance, a real friendship, or real relationship is based on having respect for each other and living in mutually beneficial states not dependent ones.

The fifth is being in a one way relationship where you are clinging on to something that is not real or something that you want and they are out to exploit that. In everything that you do, if you don't want to be a victim, you need to develop strength. There are loads of people out there that get manipulated from the simplest reason that they do not want to be alone. And so rather than face the prospect of solitary living, they allow themselves to be manipulated just so that they have somebody around them.

The sixth thing you have to be cognizant of to be able to avoid or extricate yourself from a manipulative situation is the voice of your heart. One of the things that most people forget is that they actually know what is going on. They just chose to bury their head in the sand, or they chose to let the situation take care of itself. There is some truth to that strategy, but it doesn't come from acquiescence, it comes from driving the solution. You do not need to be confrontational to neutralize the emotional manipulation, you have to strengthen your mental state and then stand your ground.

The seventh thing that you need to look at is the external factors that are causing the hesitance in departure or repair. First of all not every situation warrants departure, breakup, otherwise some form of permanent disassociation. In some cases negotiation highlighting the problem will have a considerable impact. But you need to look at all the factors that are tripping you up. For instance mothers with kids find that breaking up will cause a problem for the kids. That's just an example to show the kinds of external issues that may be weighing you down. You need to get familiar with what those issues are so that you can isolate the kinds of reasons that are preventing the hard conversations and the possible break.

The eighth issue that you need to look at to work your way toward overcoming this situation is to keep track of each issue that is causing your discomfort. Short of outright fear, you need to look at each emotional response to the situation. You need to take the time to look at this in a way that is methodical so that you do not let a simple issue blow up into ta critical one. Your job here is to find a solution, and not to make things worse.

The ninth thing that you need to do is find the emotional leverage that is being used and neutralize it as quickly as possible. Emotional manipulation is about manipulating you from inside and that is usually connected to something. When that person finds the thing that you yield to, they have their hook to get under your skin. You need to isolate and understand the emotional trigger and neutralize that trigger before the manipulator knows what is going on. That may actually be good for both of you.

Finally, you need to seek emotional support from a neutral party that is not going to take your side but is also not going to feed the anxiety. In a long term manipulative situation, it may tough to see things on your own, but a third part may be able to be your eyes and ears. I am very against the involvement of third parties in a two party relationship because the complex dynamics are never easily explained or understood. But in the case of emotional manipulation, it can be hard to see the forest for the trees or it may be difficult to see past the baggage. This person that you chose to help you must not be emotionally vested, or must not be able to sway the situation any further than it already is.

In total there are twenty ways of looking at the possible ways someone could get to manipulating you. There are more but these are synthesized in such a way that you can use them to develop a sense of what is going in instead of giving you an exhaustive checklist that would completely be overwhelming and possibly cause you to derive the wrong conclusions for the situation that is unique to you.

Your first act should be to look at the appropriate issue – long or short term. The second would be to look at your list and then think about them in turn and see how they apply to you, if at all. The third is to look at this list and be positive about yourself. You are not a failure for being manipulated emotionally. It is a part of all of us to have fears and to have anxiety. You will see that the next chapter is dedicated to this topic and you will start to understand how your mind works and what happens when you are faced with something like this. The real and credible thing that you can do is not to give up or sink, but to strengthen your own psyche and then evaluate what you want to do from there.

Unless this is life threatening you should not try to come to conclusion harshly or in haste. If you feel like you are in mortal danger then you need to be smart about it and seek professional help.

The Role of the Manipulator's Intent

Most people want to know how to read the intent of the would be manipulator and for that I say that there is no need to do that because there is a more effective way and that is to look within yourself and see the power potential between the two. The human kind is fairly opportunistic in its ways and that can be said for all species of life on this planet. Even water is opportunistic in the way it fills holes and crevasses – it doesn't leave any spot untouched.

The role of the manipulator's intent is then wholly irrelevant because regardless of whether they intend to manipulate you or they do it unbeknownst themselves, the effect is the same. In fact those who premeditate it may be easier to talk to than the one who does it on autopilot. That's because they are so deep into it that they don't even know they are doing it; and you can't talk about something to someone who doesn't think that it exists.

But if the person's intent becomes clear because you have seen them do it to others then you don't even need to think twice before you sever the relationship. Never start anything with a person you know is manipulative. The benefit is never worth the cost in this relationship and it will tire you out. The more that launch assaults the more you are forced to defend yourself. You have no choice on the matter, you can never let a manipulator come into your mind, and so you have to power the defenses. That takes energy and time. Just fending them off can be a full time job so you don't even want to get into that position. Move on. Manipulators are not worth it.

Every relationship needs to be in balance. There is always give and take, and there is always a zero sum game for the individuals, but a net gain for the couple. Let me explain. A balanced relationship is one that sees equitable contribution from both sides where party A gives the same as party B. There is no net gain. But as a whole, when you put it together Group AB (consisting of Party A and B) is no greater than the sum of the parts.

That is a normal relationship. It is mutually respectful and mutually beneficial.

But in a manipulative relationship (this is not limited to couples – it can be any relationship) one party contributes more and loses more without getting nothing in return and the sum of the two is less than the parts. This is not only a manipulative situation, and one that results in a net loss, but one that is bordering on abusive (psychologically).

That is the reason that emotionally manipulative relationships should never be encouraged, pursued, continued or tolerated. They should be terminated without mercy and without regret. If a person allows you to manipulate them, then you should look to getting out of that relationship, and if a person is manipulating you, then you should get out of that relationship as well.

No good will come from it and the tools to getting out are simple – recognize it and outwit it by strengthening your own psyche.

The one thing that you should know however is that the core of the manipulator's intent is made up of instilling fear into their victims. They do this with full knowledge of their intention, or they do it unintentionally. If you can understand your fears then you can overcome any form of manipulation. That is the subject for the next chapter.

Chapter 4:
The Psychology of Fear in Manipulation

We are born with fear within us. It is a chemical, genetic, and physiological state that works to keep us alive. Remember that one of the purposes we possess inherently is survival. Fear promotes survival by changing our physiological state from one o rest to one of high alert.

There is fear involved in everything we do; some we feel intensely, others mildly, and some even result in no perceptible response.

Fear is a deep subject and it is at the heart of almost everything we do. No matter how confident we are, or how strong, fear is pervasive and ever present – the only difference between one situation and the next is the degree of fear.

Before we get further into it, it will be best if we took a serious look at the components of fear and the severity of the various degree of fear so that we can identify it, its triggers, the way we respond to it, and if we can find that profile and identify it, we can then pinpoint the events that lead toward manipulation. Why?

Because fear is the tool that keeps victims paralyzed. This paralysis first removes resistance to the manipulation, then goes on to alter the mind in a way that affects the way they see themselves.

It will be clear as we deconstruct the essence of fear.

Fundamentals of Fear

Fear describes certain emotional, psychological and physiological states. We sometime use the term fear when we intend to describe anxiety, phobia or even being scared. However, to be accurate, fear is more the physiological response to the comprehensive input of the various faculties within the brain when it is presented with stimulus happening externally (or internally) – perceived or real, that would result in a certain hazard.

In simpler terms here's what we need to look out for:

- Comprehensive Input

- Cerebral Faculties

- Perceived or Real Stimulus

- Hazard

Comprehensive Input

When professionals talk about comprehensive input, they are trying to convey that the mind is more than one single entity, but instead, it is made up of a countless number of physical and functional areas. They are not something that can be individually identified and extricated easily. It's not like a hard drive and a processor in a computer that you can look under the hood and it's all neatly arranged. . Comprehensive input is built over the experiences of a life time and from genetic inheritance. Take for instance a child who has never been burnt by a flame before. No matter how much you explain the pain of being singed to that child, that child is not going to fully understand it until he or she experiences it themselves. The experience is complex. There are different kinds of pain, different periods of consequence, there is a change in the perception of fire – which until then has been good from a distance. The input is complex and comprehensive.

The combined response to this, or any stimuli, involves various parts of our mind, i.e. memory of pleasure & pain, experiences of detriment, ability to visualize consequences, even to imagine, all come into play. It is the compilation of these responses that act as a cascade heading toward our fear center. When the threshold is overwhelmed, the symptoms of fear kick in.

Anxiety is intimately related to fear and is part of the whole manipulation process. You will have unground tremor feeling – as in its there but barely perceptible. Your anxiety is a flag that tells you that something is not right and that something beneath the surface is happening but you just can't detect the epicenter of the problem. Most victims of manipulation get this after a while but they brush it off and the symptoms manifest in physical issues – migraine, anxiety, breakouts, early onset of menopause, loss of sexual appetite and so on.

This is a little different than the symptoms of fear which are significantly more proactive and urgent in the response that manifests. The onset of anger, hatred, and the energy to run or the irritation to fight are more attuned to a person who is already aware of the manipulation but has no power to stop it.

Cerebral Faculties

Your brain is just tissue supplied with oxygen and nutrients. It has a specific function just like your heart, kidneys, or lungs. But beware in thinking that the brain and the mind are the same. They are not. The brain is a physical object, and thereby tangible, whole the mind is a concept and therefore intangible. The mind requires a functioning brain to perform, the brain does not need a functional mind to survive.

Your physical brain is made up of four distinguishable areas: the brainstem; the limbic system; the cerebellum; and, the cerebrum. Research has proven the evolution of the brain and we now that it started with the brainstem - that's the part that sits at the base of your skull and is attached to spine, which was the first to form.

Subsequently, the limbic system came about – and this was over the course of thousands of generations. This limbic system sits on top of the brainstem and is tasked with homeostasis – the responsibility to maintain the body in balance. Take perspiration for instance – it is a homeostatic function designed to cool the body when it exceeds normal operating temperatures.

It turns out that our fear center is also located here and that is why many of the homeostatic functions tend to activate when we experience fear – sweating, heavy breathing, dilated pupils, etc.

Fear evolved at that time as a defense mechanism for all species – even trees have it but it is controlled differently. All animals and creatures have fear centers and it is almost always located in the same approximate area relative to the strata of the brain. You need fear to survive. It gives you the boost of strength like nitrous oxide does to a race car without it; you will not be able to ramp up the needed strength to fight or to flee.

Fear and anxiety, are good things when kept in control and understood. If you are the subject of manipulation, anxiety is the warning sign; fear is the call to action.

From modern neuroscience we know beyond any doubt that the fear center has influence and control over other areas of the brain. It can instruct the brain stem control involuntary acts, it can prepare the body for enhanced performance or it can just cut of all movement - like when a child freezes in fear, or a dear, in headlights.

As such, we realize that fear can cause one of three possible outcomes: fight; flight, or freeze. Freezing is a very important aspect of self-preservation. It may not be totally useful in modern contexts for the human species, but if you think about the predator-prey dynamic, you will see that much of the predators had eyesight that relied on contrast and movement. So if something was still, it didn't really get noticed.

That was the reason for naturally freezing and we still have that today. Remember we may have developed different physical forms from our ancestors, but the brain that we possess is the result of evolution across a longer period of time. This the reasons we freeze when faced with a situation that raises fear in us.

Freezing also applies to us when we are totally aware of the manipulation. The freeze here is one that straddles indecision. One dimension we are uncertain of our own feelings of fear. The second is that we do not want to rock the cart, because a known inequity is better than an unknown consequence. The third is we languish while we allow more evidence to pile up or the situation to change. Manipulation can change for the better, but it can also get worse. Until you have more information where it is going, your situation is precarious.

Back to the brain.

As the brain evolved, more sophistication built on top of the primal brain. Take for instance the appreciation of art. The taste, ability to interpret and the refined aspects of subtle variances in art and taste reside in the neo cortex, the latest addition to the brain. It is the neo cortex that gives us sophistication that those with lesser portions do not have. But the primal and the contemporary versions of your brain are connected. That connection now results in more sophisticated versions of fear and anxiety.

For this reason, anxiety and fear can impair our ability to analyze and our judgment. The centers to analyze and adjudicate are actually fine, but it gets blocked by the fear center. The fear and the resolution of that fear become the highlight. Needless worry followed by the resolution of that worry form a habit of intoxicating pleasure. That pleasure creates a habit so much so that the body starts to deal in the habit of worry and resolution rather than dealing with the underlying problem.

Fear also has control of the brains punishment and reward mechanism so that it creates a habit to obey the limbic system rather than to override it. This has to do with habits and what you will find is that over time anxieties get worse because the limbic system rewards us to behave in that way. It's like having ice cream when we know we shouldn't.

Be aware that the part of you that is reading and assimilating the information in this book is part of the neo cortex and because the old and the new parts of the brain are hardwired, being overwhelmed in the neo cortex can trigger the fear centers of the bran – ever feel that you are afraid when you are overwhelmed? On the other hand, this nature of being hardwired on top of each other also has a reverse effect. When you get overwhelmed in other areas of the neo cortex, it tends to trigger your limbic system and you start to activate the fear responses of your primal brain.

The state of the modern man is not one where he fears a predator beast on a daily basis, but rather he has other elements of his life that tend to overwhelm him and tend to threaten other centers of his existence and present hazards that activate the fear center of the brain.

The reverse is also true. Because of this hardwired state, being overwhelmed in other areas of the neo cortex, seems to activate the fear centers of the limbic system. So modern man does not just have the fear centers activated when a wolf attacks, he also triggers symptoms of fear when other areas of his life threaten a negative consequence. You will see this as the elements of fear are listed out later in the book.

Manipulators are good at using these natural fears when getting control of their victims. They place them in untenable positions and then extract their benefit while making the victim feel that that is the best way forward.

When we refer to cerebral faculties, we are not talking about the structural sections of the brain as much as we are referring to the functional aspects of the mind. Mental faculties are not something totally physical like the brain. They are power centers of the brain that result from the combination of evolution, experience, teaching and conditioning. One of our most powerful centers is the ability to reason and rationalize. This is opposed to our ancient faculty of fear.

Perceived or Real Stimulus

If you recall, the next factor in the clinical definition of fear is stimuli – real or perceived. Stimuli, whether real or perceived, refers to anything that automatically has an impact and evokes a response, whether it is physically acted out, or just imperceptibly felt.

A joke is a kind of stimuli that causes laughter; a child's nightmare, although wholly imagined, is a stimulus that triggers a real sense of fear. Fear is oblivious to whether the stimuli are real or imagined. If you sit down long enough and imagine the most fearful thing, you will experience fear.

When relevant stimuli is presented, the fear center of the brain is activated and initially puts the fight or flight responses on standby. The body receives a rush of adrenaline, pores open, pupils dilate, and blood pressure increases - all the things you need to fight, or to flee the scene.

In manipulation the offensive act does not rise to the level of imminent danger and so fear is not triggered in the same way, but more in a way that leaves you incapacitated from indecision as you are left guessing. The indecision and the hint of something wrong affect the neo cortex and overwhelm it and that triggers the fear center.

But there is one problem with this logic thus far - what has all this got to do with manipulation? Manipulation is about the use of this fear and this indecision that allows the aggressor to reach within the victim and use that fear to his advantage.

The pallet of fear stretches over five distinct elements. When you understand this, you will be able to better understand your response to manipulation. These elements of fear are called hazards.

Hazard

This element needs some differentiation from the discussion of stimuli. There are five main hazards that sit at the core of fear. It stays regardless of upbringing, social values, culture. In short, it is common to every human being.

Existential

The first main hazard is any form of existential threat. Our minds are designed to protect our life and existence so that we can propagate our species – remember that that is the purpose of life. When you hear about the science of evolution, natural selection, food chain, and survival of the fittest, well this is nature's way to counterbalance life on earth.

If gazelles in the Savannah had no fear, then fight or flight won't kick in when a lion pursues, and they will be devoured without a chase or a fight. Eventually, all the gazelles will be dead, and because of a lack of prey, the lions will be dead too. This logic is simplistic, but it's valid nonetheless. Fear keeps life alive and in balance. The basis of fear here is self-preservation, which in turn is responsible for the longevity of the species and by extension, biodiversity. But used incorrectly, fear can be misunderstood and manipulated to affect us. This is what we have to get a grip on.

Mutilation

The second hazard is the possibility of mutilation. Mutilation or loss of limb ranks higher in terms of its ability to evoke fear. Mutilation also covers things like being mauled by a bear, or bitten by a dog, or even stung by a bee.

Freedom

The third is the loss of freedom. The pain of this loss is long lasting and those with even the slightest imagination find the pain unbearable and thus the fear is even higher. This freedom is not just the act of being kidnaped or imprisoned. It even includes the fear of losing the ability to walk. An acute sense of claustrophobia, as an example, arises from this. It can even be the loss of freedom due to financial wherewithal. It is possible to be manipulated into things but accepting it because the lifestyle is good.

Social Abandonment

The fourth is the hazard of social abandonment. We are social animals and require the collaboration and companionship of society to exist. Social abandonment is a precursor to extinction and it is a powerful fear factor. Separation anxiety reflects such a situation, or event getting used to the aggressor can be a cause for manipulation when the thought is that the victim will lose the ability to see the person again.

Ego

The final and most potent hazard that ignites fear is the death of the ego. This is more so in humans because of the existence of the ego in the human species than in less evolved animals. However, the ego is deeply ingrained in the human and is complex. It manifests in everyone differently. Fear of the death of ego is unfathomable to the average mind.

Every other fear, phobia, and anxiety that you can think of is a derivation of one or a combination of these five hazards. The intensity can also vary and it can sometimes be real or perceived.

Fear and Manipulation

Fear arises because of manipulation and fear can give rise to manipulation. The human condition is built on a hierarchy. We see that in insects and animals. Have you ever seen a pack of wolves devour their prey? The Alpha male is the first to eat and once he is done, the rest start to attack the carcass in a pre-established pecking order. The weakest one is the last one to eat. This is the wolf that is the least aggressive and most afraid and because of this comparative level of fear and strength, the weaker one is dominated. It is a path of all things that live.

Fear exhibited by an individual is not only the cause of manipulation, it is also the reason for manipulation. And that is the reason that a person who is being manipulated needs to come to the truth on their own and the person who is looking in from the outside needs to be very delicate with how they handle it and assign blame. The last thing you want to do is place the blame on the aggressor. In some situations, that would actually weaken the victim even more.

As you go through this book and you bring to mind the other areas of manipulation we have talked about, remember also that the foundation fears on the five things we referred to as Hazards in the last chapter: existence, mutilation, freedom, society, and ego. On top of that add the framework of Intent, Relationship and Gravity and you see that the manipulation of a person is best handled by the actors in the following order:

1. Victim

2. Aggressor and victim

3. Aggressor

The highest priority in solving the manipulative situation is to be able to recognize yourself as the victim and empower your mind and spirit to break its grip. That means it is the victim that needs to stand up to it and understand their own position and role and take back the power the aggressor has over the victim The simplest way to look at it is to look at the list above. The person who is the most responsible and the person who is the most responsible for your happiness is you. The person most responsible for your safety is you and you have all you need to bring that to fruition. The only thing that is stopping you is you remind set and that has become a habit. You need to reverse that habit and you need to be able to snatch the power back for yourself. We look at how to get out of manipulation in the next chapter.

Chapter 5: Beliefs, Habits and overcoming Manipulation

The bricks and mortar in the analogy which are built on the foundation are the beliefs that you come to learn, experience and figure out. It is learns, one brick at a time, from the things you observe growing up, it's the things you hear your parents and other influential people say, it's the books you read and the movies you watch. All these form an intricate web of beliefs that thicken over time.

Beliefs

Beliefs are not easily disposed of, but when they are altered, they change a wide array of things in one's life. Like breaking down a wall and making an extension. You can't demolish that wall with everyday activity, you've got to get a sledgehammer and use muscle to bring it down.

On top of the bricks and mortar, in the analogy, comes plaster. In the psyche, this refers to thoughts. Thoughts tend to reflect the state of the brick and mortar underneath. If the brick is laid evenly, the plaster goes on evenly, masking minor variations, but exposing major ones.

Thoughts are what circulate in the conscious realm in your head. It's what you 'hear'. It is the 'voice' of your beliefs, presented in terms your conscious mind comprehends - most likely it manifests in your primary language, and it uses the vocabulary you most commonly engage in. If you use positive imagery, positive language, you can be fairly certain that your thoughts will also be positive. If you are prone to exaggeration, your language will also be bombastic.

On top of the plaster, comes paint - the building's equivalent of the psyche's facade. This is the part that gives rise to duality, sometimes even forms the beginnings of split personality (although there is more to that). The facade is where we say things we don't really mean. Times when we say 'Good Morning' even when we feel like it's a lousy day. Or when we compliment something unsightly. The facade alters with the outside environment and is designed to bridge the person with the environment.

The subconscious of the human psyche (continuing with the house analogy) is everything from the foundation to the plaster, excluding the paint and the voice in your head. You can't directly see, hear, feel or touch the subconscious. But without it your persona and your psyche would not exist efficiently.

We hear the term 'subconscious mind' every time we pick up material related to psychology. Sometimes it's really elusive to pin down the actual meaning, but trying to explain the world of the subconscious is a topic of an entirely separate book or volume of books. For our purposes, in getting to the bottom of fear, it will suffice to say that the subconscious mind is the crucial "behind the scenes" processes that have significant impact on our attitudes, moods, behaviors, personality, choices and such.

The subconscious is a valuable part of our existence. You just can't observe it with your senses. If you want to see what your subconscious is doing, you have to go about it differently - you have to partake in something called reflection - specifically Introspective Reflection. Reflection is where we look for clues into our subconscious. We will look at this in the next chapter.

As we move from the subconscious to the surface, we communicate with other living organisms - including other humans, animals and plants. Our communication with them is a function of what we believe inside (expressed by thoughts). Our communication takes the form of words (in any language) and when those words are repeated enough times, it causes a feedback loop into our own psyche whereby our actions will soon tend towards our words.

This is one of the reasons, positive reinforcement works so well, and so do negative ones.

Habits

Habits are neither good nor bad. They are just the mind's way to automate and shift some of the processing burden away from the conscious mind. Remember, the conscious mind is rather limited in capacity. The conscious mind is extremely capable of processing and handling one thing at a time.

Habits have three parts to it: a trigger; an act; and, a reward.

Imagine a trigger to be an event where someone gives you something; you respond with something your parents taught you to do, which is to say 'thank you' - the act; this results in you feeling good and seeing the appreciation in the presenter's eyes. That's your reward. After the first, second, third time, the act of saying 'thank you' becomes a habit.

Fear can become a habit as well. So can anxiety. So can phobias. So can crying. Once it becomes a habit, you have one additional area of your mind that you have to deal with to change. Be careful of what you do repeatedly, because it gets worse if it becomes a habit. If you act in a certain way, which will eventually become a habit.

Once something becomes a habit, and it continues, it becomes who you are. It pervades the realm of just being an action, and now becomes part of your value system. When a habit is repeated enough times, it penetrates to the foundation and becomes part of your ego. This becomes harder to change, but not impossible.

In many instances failure is a habit. When habit combine with fear, and their common goal is failure, there is no way your conscious mind will ever overcome it. It will trip you up at every step.

The reason it becomes harder is because once something gets past your conscious thought and down to your foundation, it becomes subconscious and you can't pinpoint it without the help of a psychiatrist or by deep introspection and reflection. That is what we are going to teach you to do here.

You are very much in control of your destiny. If you think it's fear that's tripping you up, then get ready to break those shackles. Because if you don't then those skewed, fear-tainted values and actions, will hijack your destiny.

Reflection

To tackle fear, habits, and the manipulation, your first move is to understand its source in you, then understand its implications, followed by what, if any, you have to alter, to arrive at your desired outcome. There is only one way to do this - reflection.

Let's give the idea reflection a little light. To reflect on something is to think deeply about it. When you think deeply, it means that you need to think past what is superficial and look deeper. Since you can't detect the processes of your subconscious mind, you have to deduce its motivation and its design from the thoughts and actions that manifest from it.

To be introspective, means to look at something inside. When we put them together, what Reflection means is to take a hard look at the thoughts that go through your mind, the actions that you commit and the resulting forces that act on your life.

Detecting your fear profile is best approached from Reflection, because it gets you to look hard at the consequences of your actions and your thoughts. But you can't just change your thoughts overnight, and even if you tried forcing yourself to change the way you think, it wouldn't work - at least not for long.

To really change your destiny, you have to change your actions, as well. And to do that you have also to change your actions and your patterns. Of course you could superficially change your words by consciously drafting and editing what you say on the fly. But that would be insincere. Insincerity would place a heavier burden on you and restrict your chance of success.

But the problem with going anywhere deeper than your thoughts, as mentioned earlier, is that the language and mode of communication changes. Your subconscious does not speak your same language. In fact your subconscious communicates with you in a binary language and it's hard to decipher when you merely glance at it. To make any sense of it requires deep Reflection.

How to Conduct Reflection

Reflection should be conducted once a day, every day at a specific time of day – so as to create a habit. It is preferable to do it before you sleep at night, but more importantly it should be done in solitude without any distractions.

Begin by relaxing and looking back at the events of your day and the events that involved the aggressor. Since you already know the five hazards, try to draw a straight line from the permission you give to be manipulated to one (or more) of the Hazards. Use your imagination. Ask hard questions. Take responsibility for the catastrophe. But do it without feeling guilt or fault.

Don't be disappointed if you do not seem to make any progress the first few times. Keep at it.

Reflection will eventually start to pay off as you begin to instinctively see the correlation of events of manipulation and your subconscious fear triggers. When you start to make headway, it will be in the form of being able to identify which Hazard(s) corresponds to which fear. What you will eventually see is that there is a pattern. Most people, by the time they hit thirty, have established their subconscious fear patterns.

Face Your Fears

Once you get into the routine of Reflection you will find that thoughts will pop into your head at other times of the day. It is just the revelations of your inner mind. Take note of those. As you begin to recognize your Hazards and their corresponding fears, it is time for you to look at them rationally and determine if there is any mortal danger in them. If there aren't, take the plunge and confront your fear.

If you are afraid of heights, go bungee jumping, or skydiving. If you are afraid of snakes, go to a petting zoo and pet a non-poisonous snake. Push your limits of fear. What do you do when you have no strength to lift a heavy object? You go to the gym and build your muscles by doing the exact thing that you found you can't do – but you do them in increments. Facing manipulation is the same way. You face your fears in increments and successes. Until one day you are able to set yourself free.

The key to attacking manipulation is taking action. Fear creates a standoff in our minds, regardless of the Hazards that are responsible for them. When fear kicks in, it trips us up and we feel weak and that weakness leads us to being manipulated.

Power of your Subconscious

Communication coming from the subconscious is binary in nature. It either rewards you for the right answer or punishes you. When you get it right, you feel good, when you get it wrong, you get that nagging feeling. It's as simple as that. You've had it before; it's just that you keep calling it "that nagging feeling' or some would say instinct.

Reflection takes practice. You have to keep doing it over and over until you get the hang of it. All - without exception - highly successful people do it regularly. What all this have to do with fear?

What you think you are afraid of, is most likely not the complete picture. To get the complete picture, or your complete fear profile, you need to engage in Reflection. You need to practice Reflection to the point that Reflection is constantly running in the background, parallel in everything you do - yes that's right - subconsciously, like a habit.

Most people don't really know what they fear and what they land up doing is being afraid of the unknown - in this case, they are afraid of the fear. The reason FDR said, "Nothing to fear but fear itself" becomes more evident in this light. The most feared of all fears is the fear of uncertainty. Because when you are faced with uncertainty, any one, combination or all the hazards could be lurking, we just don't know. And so what do we instinctively do, we run for the hills (flight), we do nothing and fall into depression (freeze) or we resort to self-destruction, anger and abuse (fight). See how it manifests - fight, flight and freeze.

To avoid all this, your one and only remedy, prevention and safeguard is to be in constant Reflection.

To illustrate, let's assume there is a person who is suffering from the fear of commitment. If we look at the hazards, there is no hazard resembling commitment. So what does this mean? It means that the fear of commitment is a composite - it's a combination of different fears rolled into one. Here are a few examples of composite fears.

Manipulation is a Manifestation of Fear

Fear is a condition best approached when cold. That means, attempting to resolve it in the midst of a manifestation (a panic attack or bout of anxiety) is not the right time. During those times you need to handle the symptoms.

The fear that needs to be confronted is really the fruit of the five hazards that everyone possesses in varying degrees. Those do not manifest or present in a physical feeling on a regular basis. Many times, when it does present it presents as a worry.

This worry is the resonant energy of the Hazard. In small doses, it is manageable. But manifestations of Hazards do not stay in small doses for long. They tend to compound and grow larger over time. When the Hazard inside begins to exceed the person's ability to contain it, it manifests outwardly.

The outward manifestation could be in many forms, and not all of it is directly distinguishable by the person. In some, it manifests as eating disorders. In others it manifests as self-destructive behavior or possibly destructive behavior in general. It can even fan latent anger, lead to depression, schizophrenia and other mental ailments. It can even cross the mental-physical barrier and manifest as physical diseases. Chronic headaches and migraine, cancer, suppressed immune issues, bulimia, allergies and so on.

Fear is a powerful force and has tremendous amounts of energy driving it. If we can channel that energy, it has the potential to make us stronger - remember, whatever doesn't kill you, only makes you stronger.

The Art of Dominating Your Fears

The obstacles we face in life - the ones that prevent us from reaching our dreams, and the ones that enslave us are never external – even though they may seem to be. They are always internal. All failure is our own doing. You must accept this fact. Because it is one of the most empowering truths you will ever come across. When you take responsibility for a failure, your ego will prevent you from making that mistake again.

You don't want to release your fear and walk away from it. You don't want to sweep it under the carpet. You don't want to hide it in the closet. What you have to do is confront it and beat it. You want to own your naturally installed Hazards, and deepest fears. Because when you own it, it can't affect you negatively. It can only strengthen you. That manipulator that is controlling your life is only doing so because you allow it. Short of physical harm, there is nothing they can do psychologically if you don't allow them.

To overcome your fear, you need to dominate your Hazards. To dominate your Hazards you need to observe them, observe their nature and how it affects you. You need to look for habits that have formed from them and what the triggers are. You need to study your Hazard profile and your fear profile. There is only one way to approach this, and it's through Introspective Reflection.

Take Action

Once you reflect and you slowly uncover the truth about yourself, it is time to take action against the fear. In the previous section it was written that you do the thing that you fear. From a psychological perspective what that does is prove the fear center's assumptions wrong.

In the higher functions of the mind, which is directly connected to the Hazards of the limbic system, there is an analysis of whether one has the competence to conduct a task. That competence is mostly underestimated and that then triggers the fear center into freezing. The key to overcome this is to go ahead and do the task - a small part of it. When the task is completed successfully, it shows confidence which in turn results in a little more confidence. This is one incremental step that should be followed by another. When the next task is successful, more confidence is built and that leads to taking the next higher step. This is called the competence-confidence loop.

There is one catch though. The opening position in this loop is the total lack of confidence which freezes the system and renders the person incapable of any ability to attempt. The only way to break the cycle is to take action. Once you take action, and gain competence, you can gain confidence and keep escalating until there is no fear whatsoever.

The ability to fear external threats came about to protect the species and life in general. But the world has changed. While the game of predator and prey may still play out in the Serengeti the way it did millions of years ago in the wild, the stage has changed for the human species. Fear, which was once our protection, is now, in many modern scenarios a hurdle. When fear debilitates us into inaction, it's a problem. When fear freezes us into capitulation, it's a problem. When fear shakes us, it's a problem. But we are not without recourse.

It's time to take stock of what we know and the steps to take to break the binds that have kept success at bay. Fear is a powerful force that can derail us from an otherwise stellar destiny. Everything from fear of spiders, to separation anxiety, to fear of superstitions - can be consciously debilitating, or worse, subconsciously sabotaging.

You are not successful as you want to be today because of the latent and subconscious fears you have harbored, which are anchored by the Hazards we all possess. To navigate your path to success, you need to weigh anchor. All you have to do is acknowledge their existence and move on. That's how you get over them. Acknowledge the root of the fear; analyze the assumptions, then act. If you fail the first time, act again. Keep committing the act, until success emerges.

Do not harbor fear of failure, but be afraid of not trying. The fear of failure is prospective - it's something that 'MAY' happen in the future, but it is debilitating your present. To break what may happen later, act now.

Repurpose that fear. Instead of allowing fear to freeze you, fear not giving it your all. Fear inaction. Fear complacency. But remember that you now know the one and only counter attack to fear - action. Take action to counter ego death. Take action to counter all the Hazards and you will find that each time you do, your confidence increases.

Fear, it turns out, when balanced, is a powerful ally in the game of survival. So if you think you've got a fear problem, turn it into strength and do exactly what you fear. Elicit the aid of a coach, or a friend to guide you as you take baby steps and ascend the competence-confidence loop. It really is like riding a bike. In the grand scheme of things, there is no such thing as right and wrong - there is only consequence. So do not be afraid of making a mistake.

In the grand scheme there is no such thing as failure, there is only the failure to try. In the grand scheme of things, there is nothing to fear, except fear itself. In the grand scheme of things, you have the power to decide what controls your destiny: will it be your freedom, or your fears.

The Hazards inside you that are orchestrating your myriad of fears is based on the instinct for survival, and it is antiquated. It has no relevance to our present situation. If you don't believe that, look at the freeze instinct of the deer in the headlights. Evolution dictates that freezing would ensure survival - sure it will, if it's against a larger predator, but not a speeding truck on a dark highway. We have moved so far ahead of what the rest of the species and even ourselves have evolved that we need our rational mind to wrest control from the instinct to freeze and to fear. You cannot be that deer in the headlights, the next time opportunity presents itself. Take it, act on it, own it. Make mistakes if you have to, but you no longer need to fear it.

Once you do this no one can dictate the terms of your actions. That brings any attempt to manipulate you to an end. One you reach this point you should then stand up and forgive those who tried to manipulate you because it is your ultimate show of strength. Only the weak harbor the desire for revenge. The strong do not, and you are strong.

Conclusion

Over the course of this book we have seen the elements and profile of what it means to be emotionally manipulative and who we can see it coming and how we can detect it in our own lives. Part of the insidious nature of manipulation is that it either can't be detected or it is detected but can't be rebuffed. Both are equally problematic and it is so ingrained in the fabric of the relationship that some victims even feel they are at fault for feeling that way.

The key here that we want you take away from this book is that you are not the victim no matter how it is termed and what people say. This is not just wishful thinking or hyperbole. This is a straight fact and a way out of being manipulated. You are indeed not the victim because you can make a decision at any time you wish to throw it all away. This only works if there is no threat of physical harm to you or your loved one.

If it is purely emotional manipulation, then you need to fix the emotion that is being tugged on to manipulate you and bolster that emotion or shut it off.

You must remember the Emotional Manipulation Framework that we talked about and you need to fit the manipulation that you think is afoot in the framework. If it fits that framework then you know what your subconscious has been telling you is on the mark.

No matter what book or therapist try to diagnose, the best person to understand if you are being manipulated is you – not even the manipulator knows this as well as you. This knowledge starts with a spark deep within you. If that spark ignites you will end up doing things like you are right now, going in search of information and coming across this book. So your inclinations are already intrigued and you need to find more. That is an excellent start.

In the process of discovery, as you are in now, it is best to look inside without any shadow of guilt. Guilt will do you no good and will only serve as fodder for the manipulator. You need to be guiltless but look within. Most people do not advocate looking within and nobody wants to look inside to find their strength because they mistakenly believe that looking within victimizes the person even more. It doesn't. It empowers you.

It empowers you to admit that you were weak and now you are in the way to being strong. It empowers you to admit that you were once mistaken but now you are on your way to being smarter. It empowers you to admit that you were manipulated but now you have learnt. This admission is not one that you make to others; this confession is one that you make to yourself during serious bouts of reflection.

Strength doesn't come from avoidance; strength comes from facing things head on. If you face it head on, you will find that it is quicker, cleaner and less damaging than if you let it fester and buildup.

The time you spend in reflection shouldn't be measured in years or months. It should just takes days of a couple of weeks to get your thoughts in order and to then get your ducks in a row before you confront the person you think is manipulating you.

You have two ways of going about his. You can either confront them in a confrontational way, or you could go about it with grace and poise. I prefer the later to the former. The later shifts the power dynamic and at the same time reduces the impact of expectations.

While your primary motivation is to extricate and terminate the series of manipulations, it is not your goal to escalate tensions. You may not care to be friends or be in a relationship with tis person any loner, but don't make it hostile. It doesn't help anyone.

At the same time, you do not want to change the tables on the other person. You do not want to be the one who ends up manipulating them because they're now so sorry that they did it without fully realizing what they were doing. Remember it is never a good thing to manipulate anyone, and it is never a good thing to be manipulated by anyone.

In closing, remember to take some time away and time off from the person you think is manipulating you while you analyze the situation. Go away for a while. Take a trip, go back to your parent's place, do something and don't see this person or don't communicate with this person so that you can vacate your mind of any of the thoughts that have become habitual.

There are a couple of good places in the California Mountains that offer a respite in the form of quiet retreats. They are non-denominational and they are a great place for you to sit with nature and be at peace with yourself. You will be very surprised with what you find. There is nothing more empowering than finding yourself in the midst of pristine sounds and profound silence.

Return to your own innocence and you will find the strength to be who you are without the emotional baggage of allowing emotional manipulation in your life.

Your Free Gift

Improve your Social Skills for Success

As a way of saying thanks you for your support, I wanted to grant you a special gift a free E-book called "How to Master Your Social Skills For Success".

Within this comprehensive guide you will find information on how to influence people behavior in your favor and all of the obvious and not so obvious best practices to improve your social skills. Think of this guide as your key to influence others for your own success and happiness.

You can find your free GIFT Here:

https://readingsecrets.lpages.co/lewisfischer